S0-BSO-529

Contents

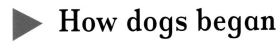 # How dogs began

Thousands of years ago there were no dogs.

People lived in families, in caves. Wolves lived in packs, in the wild.

People began to feed some of the wolves. Wolves and people hunted together for food.

OXFORD

WILD READS

Dogs

Marjorie Newman

OXFORD
UNIVERSITY PRESS

This book belongs to:

OXFORD
UNIVERSITY PRESS

Great Clarendon Street, Oxford OX2 6DP
Oxford University Press is a department of the University of Oxford.
It furthers the University's objective of excellence in research, scholarship,
and education by publishing worldwide in

Oxford   New York

Auckland   Cape Town   Dar es Salaam   Hong Kong   Karachi
Kuala Lumpur   Madrid   Melbourne   Mexico City   Nairobi
New Delhi   Shanghai   Taipei   Toronto

With offices in

Argentina   Austria   Brazil   Chile   Czech Republic   France   Greece
Guatemala   Hungary   Italy   Japan   Poland   Portugal   Singapore
South Korea   Switzerland   Thailand   Turkey   Ukraine   Vietnam

Oxford is a registered trade mark of Oxford University Press
in the UK and in certain other countries

Text © Marjorie Newman
Illustrations © Michael Langham Rowe
The moral rights of the author have been asserted

Database right Oxford University Press (maker)

This edition 2009

British Library Cataloguing in Publication Data

Data available

ISBN: 978-0-19-911971-4

1 3 5 7 9 10 8 6 4 2

Printed in China
Paper used in the production of this book is a natural,
recyclable product made from wood grown in sustainable forests.
The manufacturing process conforms to the environmental
regulations of the country of origin.

The wolves became part of the family.

Over hundreds of years, these wolves began to look different from wolves in the wild. They began to look more like dogs.

Their noses changed.

| wolf | dog (Collie) | dog (Fox terrier) |

Their ears changed.

| wolf | dog (mongrel) | dog (Basset hound) |

Their legs began to look different.

wolf

dog
(Spaniel)

dog
(Pug)

Even their tails changed.

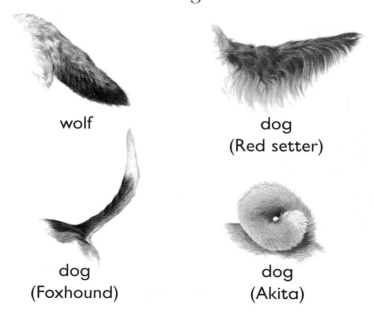

wolf

dog
(Red setter)

dog
(Foxhound)

dog
(Akita)

▶ Do dogs still behave like wolves?

There are some things which dogs have never stopped doing since the wolf-pack days.

Dogs eat fast.
Wolves eat fast.
In the wolf-pack,
a slow eater will not
get enough food to
keep it alive.

Dobermann
pinscher

Dogs bury bones to keep them safe.
Wolves bury food to keep it safe.
Any left-over food will be eaten up
by other animals.

Wolf pack and its leader

Dogs follow a leader. Wolves follow a leader. In the wolf-pack, the strongest, wisest wolf is leader.

Today you must be pack leader for your dog.

Golden retriever and its leader

► Different kinds of dogs

Today there are over 200 different breeds of dog.

Poodle

Boxer

Dalmatian

Bulldog

Corgi

Airedale terrier

Borzoi

Yorkshire
terrier

11

What dogs need

All dogs need the same things.
They need the right food – they need
meat; dog meal or biscuits; and fresh
water. It's also good to add rice, fish,
fruit and raw carrots.

Dogs need a safe, warm bed like
a basket or cardboard box with
a cosy blanket.

They need to play.
They need exercise to keep fit.

Beagle
puppies
playing

They need to be groomed. Dogs should be combed and brushed every day. They should be bathed if they get really dirty. Some dogs need regular haircuts!

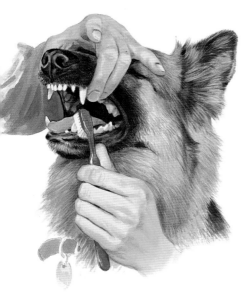

Only an adult should clean an Alsatian's teeth!

Did you know...
Cakes, sweets and chocolates are very bad for dogs.

They need a collar, lead and identity tag. They need their human family and should never be left alone for hours and hours. They need training and they need to be loved.

▶ How dogs talk to you

Dogs have their own language.
They growl and howl. They whine
and whimper, bark and yelp.

A sick or unhappy dog may whine.
A playful or happy dog may bark.
An angry dog may growl.

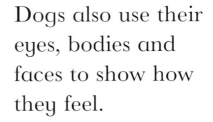

Dogs also use their
eyes, bodies and
faces to show how
they feel.

This dog is happy.

Rough
collie

Did you know…
The more you know about the way a dog
is feeling, the easier it is to train him.

This dog
is angry.

This dog
is sad.

This dog
is afraid.

Dogs can tell how **you** feel too.
They watch your body and face
and know if your voice is happy,
sad or cross.

▶ Training dogs

Dogs can be trained at almost any age, but it's best to start when a puppy is about three months old. Training can be done at home or at a dog club.

Chow chow

Dogs learn fastest when they get a reward like a titbit or a pat every time they do something right.

Good dog training

 Training must be fun for the dog.

🐾 Don't train for more than ten minutes.
Stop before that if the dog gets tired.
Two minutes is long enough for a
puppy.

🐾 When the dog does something right,
sound really pleased.

🐾 Never hit a dog that isn't doing what
you ask. You will muddle it. Just say
NO! and try again.

🐾 Remember – a frightened, unhappy
dog cannot learn.

Very important!

🐾 Never shout at a dog after it has come
to you, no matter how long it took.
It will think you are shouting at it for
coming. Next time it won't come.

17

Some ideas for training a dog

Come

1 Say, 'Rover, come!'

2 When it comes, hold the dog's collar.

3 Give the dog a titbit. Say, 'good dog.'

Jack Russell terrier

18

Sit

Hold a titbit
...t to the dog.

2 Say, '**Rover, sit!**' Move the titbit back over the dog's head. The dog will sit.

3 Give it the titbit. Say, '**good dog.**'

Lie Down

When the dog is sitting, ...y, '**Rover! Lie down!**'

... Move the titbit down ...wards the floor.

3 The dog will lie down. Give it the titbit. Say, '**good dog.**'

Special things about dogs

There are special things about all dogs.

1 Smelling

Dogs are very good at smelling. A dog can sniff out things that have been hidden.

Springer spaniel

2 Hearing

Dogs are very good at hearing. A dog can hear sounds four times further away than a person can.

Welsh corgi

Did you know...

A dog can pick out the sound of its family's car engine from any other car engine?

3 Seeing

Most dogs are not very good at seeing. They see only black, white, and grey, but are quick to see movement.

Bearded collie

4 Panting

Dogs don't sweat like people. They only lose heat through their tongues and foot pads. When a dog gets hot, it sticks out its tongue and pants. When it gets too hot, it can die of heatstroke. This is why dogs die in hot cars.

Red setter

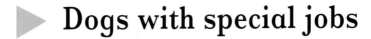 # Dogs with special jobs

Many dogs are specially trained.
Police dogs are usually Alsatians.
These dogs are quick to learn.
They can search for people and things
that are lost.

Alsatian
police dog

Guide dogs for the blind are often Labradors or Golden retrievers. They are easy to teach and like to take care of people. They wear a special harness to guide their blind owner.

Golden retriever guide dog

St Bernards are used to help find people who are buried in deep snow on the mountain.

St Bernard

Sheep dogs are often Collies. They are lively and keen to please their owner. They quickly learn to keep the sheep together.

Dogs that pull sledges are often Huskies. They can run for long distances over the snow.

Siberian huskies

Racing dogs are usually Greyhounds.
They have long legs and slim bodies.
They love to chase.

Greyhounds

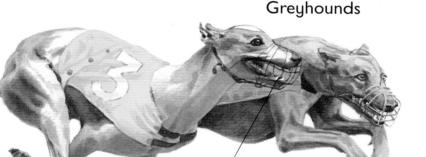

Muzzle

Acting dogs can be any breed.
They are trained to do clever things
on television or film.

Television
advertisement

▶ War dogs

Dogs have been trained to do very dangerous jobs in wartime.

In World War I, dogs carried messages to and from the trenches through all the noise and smoke of the battlefield.

Mongrel

Alsatian and parachutist

In World War II, dogs and their handlers were dropped by parachute into dangerous places. The dogs sniffed out enemy soldiers, mines and bombs.

Dogs and people

Almost any dog can make a good pet, but choose your dog carefully. Don't get a Great Dane if you live in a small flat. Don't get a Dalmatian unless you can give it lots of exercise. Don't get a Chihuahua if there are lots of big feet in your house!

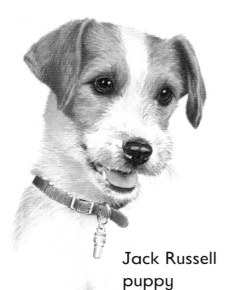

Dogs make good friends. They love to be part of the family, just like the wolves from long ago.

Jack Russell puppy

Amazing dog facts

The St Bernard is the heaviest kind of dog. One weighed over 100 kilograms.

The Saluki is the fastest kind of dog. It can run at 43 miles per hour. That's much faster than the speed at which most cars drive in towns.

The Irish wolfhound is the tallest kind of dog. It can be as tall as a five-year-old child!

The Chihuahua is the smallest kind of dog. It is as small as a man's hand.

Saluki   St Bernard   Chihuahua   Irish wolfhound

► Glossary

 breed A breed means a kind of dog. **10**

 groom When you groom an animal you smarten it. **13**

 harness A harness is a set of straps which go round an animal's body. **23**

 leader The leader is a person or animal that is followed by others. **9**

 muzzle This is like a tiny cage which goes over a dog's nose and mouth. This stops them from biting. **25**

pack A pack is a group of animals. **4, 8, 9**

 train To train a dog means to teach it how to behave.
13-14, 16-19, 22, 25-26

OXFORD

WILD READS

WILD READS will help your child develop a love of reading and a lasting curiosity about our world. See the websites and places to visit below to learn more about dogs.

Dogs

WEBSITES
http://www.learnwithdogs.co.uk/

http://www.findoutaboutdogs.com/

http://www.rspca-education.org.uk/

PLACES TO VISIT
Crufts
This dog show takes place in March every year at the NEC in Birmingham.
http://www.crufts.org.uk/

Battersea Dogs Home
http://www.dogshome.org/